A Senior's Quickie

Intro To Crypto Currency

Keith W. Coble

I

Welcome to *A Senior's Quickie Intro to Crypto currency*, your easy, no-nonsense guide to understanding the basics of digital money. You've probably heard terms like "Bitcoin" or "blockchain" and wondered, *What's this all about, and should I care?*

This book is here to give you a quick, clear picture of what cryptocurrency is, why people are talking about it, and how it might fit into your life. Even if you're just curious! No confusing jargon, no pressure to invest. Just simple, practical information to help you decide if cryptocurrency is something you want to explore.

Let's dive into the fascinating world of digital currency, made easy for you.

IV

DEDICATION

Dedicated to seniors everywhere, who continue to learn, grow, and inspire the generations that follow. May this guide help you navigate the digital world with confidence and curiosity.

To the teachers, mentors, and loved ones who showed me that no matter our age, we never stop learning.

ACKNOWLEDGMENTS

To all the seniors out there who continue to embrace new challenges with open minds and hearts, this book is for you. Your resilience and willingness to learn inspire me every day. May this guide serve as a helpful tool in navigating the digital world and enhancing your everyday life.

1

Introduction to Cryptocurrency

We will explore the basics of cryptocurrency, including what it is, how it works, and why it has become such a popular form of investment. By the end, you'll have a solid foundation for understanding the broader world of crypto and its potential as an investment option or Opportunity.

What is Cryptocurrency?

At its core, cryptocurrency is a digital currency that operates on a decentralized system using blockchain technology. Unlike traditional currencies issued by governments (like the US

Dollar or Euro), cryptocurrencies are not controlled by any central authority, such as a bank or government. Instead, they rely on a network of computers (nodes) to manage transactions and verify their accuracy.

Key Features:

Steps are essential for safeguarding your assets and ensuring you have control over your *Digital:* Exists only in electronic form, no physical coins or notes.

Decentralized:

Managed by a network of users (peer-to-peer system) rather than a central authority.

Secure:

Transactions are encrypted and verified through cryptography.

Transparent:

Every transaction is recorded on a public ledger (the blockchain), making it visible to everyone.

How Does Cryptocurrency Work?

Cryptocurrencies use blockchain technology to facilitate and verify transactions. The blockchain is essentially a public database where all transactions are recorded in a series of "blocks" that are linked together in a "chain." This ensures that the history of every transaction is traceable and tamper-proof.

Here's a simplified version of how it works:

Transaction: When you send cryptocurrency (Bitcoin) to someone, a transaction is created.

Verification:

The transaction is then verified by multiple computers (nodes) in the network, which check to make sure the sender has enough funds and that the transaction follows the rules of the network.

Block Creation:

Once verified, the transaction is bundled into a block, along with other transactions.

Blockchain Addition:

This block is then added to the existing blockchain, becoming a permanent part of the transaction history.

Why Has Cryptocurrency Gained Popularity?

Cryptocurrency has become popular for several reasons:

Potential for High Returns:

Early adopters of major cryptocurrencies like Bitcoin and Ethereum have seen huge returns on their investments, which has attracted new investors.

Decentralization and Freedom:

For many, cryptocurrencies represent a way to move away from traditional banking systems and government control, offering more financial autonomy.

Innovative Technology:

The blockchain technology underlying

cryptocurrencies promises to revolutionize industries like finance, supply chain management, and even healthcare, making it attractive not just as an investment but also as a cutting-edge technology.

Global Access:

Cryptocurrencies allow for easy cross-border transactions without the need for intermediaries like banks, making them a convenient solution for people in regions with limited banking access.

Popular Cryptocurrencies

Though there are thousands of cryptocurrencies, a few major ones dominate the market. Here's a quick overview of some of the most well-known:

Bitcoin (BTC):

The first and most well-known cryptocurrency, often seen as "digital gold" due to its high value and limited supply (21 million coins).

Ethereum (ETH):

More than just a currency, Ethereum is a platform that allows developers to create decentralized applications (DApps) using smart contracts. It's the backbone of much of the decentralized finance (DeFi) ecosystem.

Litecoin (LTC):

Created as a "lighter" version of Bitcoin, Litecoin processes transactions faster and with lower fees, making it ideal for smaller transactions.

Ripple (XRP):

Focuses on enabling fast and cheap cross-border payments, mainly for large financial institutions.

Stablecoins:

Cryptocurrencies like Tether (USDT) are tied to the value of traditional currencies, like the US Dollar, to reduce volatility. They're often used for transactions and saving within the crypto ecosystem.

Why People Invest in Cryptocurrency?

People invest in cryptocurrency for a variety of

reasons, including:

Potential for High Returns:

Many see cryptocurrency as a high-risk, high-reward investment. While prices can be volatile, some investors have experienced massive gains over time.

Diversification:

Cryptocurrencies are often used to diversify investment portfolios. Since they aren't directly tied to traditional financial markets, they can act as a hedge against economic downturns.

Belief in the Technology:

Some investors are passionate about blockchain technology and believe it has the potential to reshape the global financial system, making crypto investments a bet on the future.

Financial Freedom:

For those looking to avoid traditional banks, governments, or currency inflation, cryptocurrencies offer a decentralized alternative.

Cryptocurrency represents a major innovation in how we think about money, finance, and technology. It offers a decentralized, secure, and transparent way to transfer value, while the potential for high returns has drawn investors from around the globe. With a clear understanding of what cryptocurrency is and why it's popular, you're ready to explore the more practical aspects of how to invest.

2

Understanding the Risks and Rewards

While crypto can offer significant profits, it also comes with volatility and uncertainty. By understanding the balance between risk and reward, you can make more informed decisions and develop strategies to manage those risks.

Risk Factors in Cryptocurrency Investment

Cryptocurrency investments can be highly rewarding++arding, but they are also accompanied by notable risks that all investors should understand.

Volatility:

Cryptocurrencies are known for their extreme price fluctuations. It's not uncommon for a coin's value to change by 10% or more in a single day.

For example, Bitcoin has experienced several price crashes, losing over 50% of its value in some cases, before recovering later.

The volatility can lead to substantial losses if you're not prepared or if you need to sell in a downturn.

Security Risks:

Despite the security features of blockchain technology, cryptocurrency exchanges and wallets can be vulnerable to hacks.
Several high-profiled hackers in 2014, led to the loss of millions of dollars' worth of Bitcoin.

Solution: Always use strong security measures, including cold storage wallets and two-factor authentication.

Regulatory Uncertainty:

Governments worldwide are still figuring out

how to regulate cryptocurrency. Regulations can change rapidly, potentially affecting the market.

For example, China's crackdown on crypto mining and transactions in 2021 significantly impacted global prices.

Impact: Future regulations could influence how cryptocurrencies are traded, taxed, or even whether they are legal in certain countries.

Market Manipulation:

The cryptocurrency market is less regulated than traditional financial markets, making it more susceptible to manipulation by large investors (often called "whales").

Pump-and-dump schemes:

This is where the price of a cryptocurrency is artificially inflated by coordinated buying, only for the coin to be sold off quickly, leaving other investors with losses.

Technology Risks:

Since cryptocurrency is still an emerging

technology, there are risks associated with bugs, protocol changes, or technological obsolescence. For example, a security flaw in Ethereum's smart contracts could lead to the loss of funds if not properly addressed.

Potential Rewards of Cryptocurrency Investment

Though the risks are considerable, many investors are drawn to cryptocurrency because of its potential rewards.

High Returns:

Cryptocurrency investments can yield exponential returns, especially for early adopters or those holding assets long-term.

Example: Bitcoin was worth less than $1 in 2010 and reached over $60,000 in 2021. Ethereum has also seen similar rapid growth since its launch in 2015.

Caution: While early investors have made huge profits, past performance doesn't guarantee future returns.

Portfolio Diversification:

Cryptocurrencies can be a way to diversify your investment portfolio, especially because they don't always move in tandem with traditional markets. This is especially useful for investors looking to balance their portfolios with assets that behave differently from stocks, bonds, and real estate.

Decentralized Finance (DeFi) Opportunities:

The rise of decentralized finance (DeFi) allows investors to participate in staking, yield farming, and lending. These can provide additional income streams beyond simply holding crypto.

Example: Staking on Ethereum 2.0 can yield regular rewards, while platforms like Aave and Compound let users earn interest on cryptocurrency deposits.

Access to Early-Stage Innovation:

Investing in smaller or emerging cryptocurrencies allows investors to participate in potentially game-changing technology before it becomes mainstream.

Example: Those who invested in Ethereum early on got in at a time when decentralized applications (DApps) and smart contracts were in their infancy.

Balancing Risks and Rewards:

To succeed in cryptocurrency investment, it's crucial to balance risk and reward.

Here are some strategies that can help:

Diversify Your Investment:

Don't put all your money into one cryptocurrency. Spreading your investments across a few different coins can reduce the risk of significant losses.

Example: You might allocate 50% to Bitcoin, 30% to Ethereum, and the rest to smaller, emerging coins or stablecoins.

Only Invest What You Can Afford to Lose:

Due to the high risk, it's recommended to invest only a small percentage of your overall portfolio in cryptocurrency. Never invest money that you can't afford to lose.

Stay Informed:

Regularly monitor the market and any news or developments that may affect your investments. Cryptocurrencies can be sensitive to global news, such as regulatory changes or major technological upgrades.

Consider Dollar-Cost Averaging:

Instead of trying to "time the market," consider investing a fixed amount on a regular schedule (weekly or monthly). This strategy, known as dollar-cost averaging, can help smooth out the effects of market volatility.

Use Stop-Loss Orders:

On exchanges that allow it, you can set stop-loss orders that automatically sell your cryptocurrency if it falls to a certain price. This can help protect you from large losses in volatile markets.

Risk Management Tips:

Managing risk is an essential part of any investment strategy. Here are some additional tips to reduce your exposure to cryptocurrency's inherent risks:

Stay Updated on Security Practices:

Keep your wallet and accounts secure by using hardware wallets for long-term storage, avoiding public Wi-Fi for transactions, and enabling two-factor authentication (2FA) wherever possible.

Set Clear Goals and Limits:

Determine in advance how much you're willing to invest, your target return, and how much loss you're willing to accept before exiting a position.

Know the Tax Implications:

Many countries now tax cryptocurrency gains, so make sure you understand how crypto transactions will affect your tax liabilities. Not keeping track of this can lead to unexpected bills.

Cryptocurrency investing carries both risks and rewards, often in greater extremes than traditional investments. By understanding the volatility, security concerns, and potential regulations, you can prepare for the downside while still positioning yourself to take advantage of the high rewards that cryptocurrency can offer.

3

How to Get Started with Cryptocurrency Investment

Now that you understand the basics and the potential risks and rewards of cryptocurrency investment, it's time to dive into the practical steps to begin investing. In this chapter, we will guide you through setting up a cryptocurrency wallet, choosing the right exchange, and navigating the security practices essential for safe transactions.

Setting Up a Wallet

A cryptocurrency wallet is where you store your digital assets. Unlike a traditional wallet that holds physical cash, a crypto wallet stores your private keys. unique codes that grant you access to your cryptocurrencies on the blockchain.

Types of Wallets

Hot Wallets:

These are digital wallets connected to the internet, making them easily accessible but potentially more vulnerable to hacking. Examples include mobile or desktop apps like Trust Wallet, MetaMask, or wallets provided by exchanges like Coinbase.

Cold Wallets:

These wallets are offline, offering greater security since they are not susceptible to online attacks. The most common forms of cold wallets are hardware wallets like Ledger Nano or Trezor. These devices store your private keys offline, protecting them from hackers.

Paper Wallets:

Though less common, paper wallets are physical printouts of your private and public keys. They are secure from hackers but can be easily lost or damaged.

Choosing the Right Wallet:

If you're a beginner and plan on making frequent transactions, a hot wallet might be the best option due to its ease of use.
If you plan to hold large amounts of cryptocurrency long-term, a cold wallet is recommended for added security.

Many investors use both:

a hot wallet for small amounts used in daily transactions and a cold wallet for large, long-term holdings.

Choosing a Cryptocurrency Exchange

A cryptocurrency exchange is where you can buy, sell, and trade cryptocurrencies. It acts like a marketplace where you can exchange traditional currency (like USD or EUR) for cryptocurrency, or trade between different cryptocurrencies.

Types of Exchanges:

Centralized Exchanges (CEX):

These exchanges are run by companies that act as intermediaries between buyers and sellers. Popular examples include Coinbase, Binance, Kraken, and Gemini. They tend to be user-friendly but require you to trust the platform with your funds.

Decentralized Exchanges (DEX):

Unlike centralized exchanges, DEXs like Uniswap and SushiSwap allow peer-to-peer trading directly between users, without a middleman. This offers more privacy and security but may be more complex for beginners.

Key Factors to Consider When Choosing an Exchange:

Reputation and Security:

Check if the exchange has a strong reputation for security and user satisfaction. Look for features like two-factor authentication (2FA) and cold storage options for the exchange itself.

Fees:

Exchanges charge different fees for trades,

withdrawals, and deposits. Make sure to compare fees before choosing an exchange.

Ease of Use:

If you're new to cryptocurrency, user-friendly platforms like Coinbase or Binance are ideal for beginners.

Available Cryptocurrencies:

Some exchanges offer a wide range of coins and tokens, while others focus on major currencies like Bitcoin and Ethereum. Choose an exchange that supports the currencies you're interested in.

Liquidity:

Liquidity refers to how easily you can buy or sell an asset without causing significant price fluctuations. Larger exchanges tend to have higher liquidity, making it easier to trade quickly and at fair prices.

KYC (Know Your Customer) and Security Practices

Many cryptocurrency exchanges require KYC

verification, which involves providing personal information to comply with government regulations. While this might seem like a hassle, it's essential for maintaining the security and legality of the exchange. Here's what you need to know:

What is KYC?:

KYC is a process where exchanges verify the identity of their users to prevent illegal activities such as money laundering or fraud.
This process usually requires you to submit identification documents, like a passport or driver's license, and sometimes proof of address.

Why It Matters:

KYC ensures that exchanges comply with laws and regulations, protecting both the exchange and its users. While decentralized exchanges may not require KYC, they often come with more risks (like lack of support or recourse if something goes wrong).

Essential Security Practices

Given the risks associated with cryptocurrency,

particularly security risks, it's critical to follow best practices to protect your investments.

Two-Factor Authentication (2FA):

Always enable 2FA on your exchange and wallet accounts. This adds an extra layer of security by requiring a second form of verification (such as a code from your phone) in addition to your password.

Strong Passwords:

Use unique, complex passwords for your accounts. Avoid using the same password for multiple platforms. Consider using a password manager to store and manage your passwords securely.

Backup Your Wallet:

Always back up your wallet, especially if you're using a cold wallet. Most wallets will give you a recovery phrase (also called a seed phrase). Keep this phrase somewhere safe and offline. If you lose your recovery phrase, you could lose access to your cryptocurrency forever.

Avoid Public Wi-Fi:

When accessing your exchange or wallet, avoid using public Wi-Fi networks. Hackers can exploit insecure networks to steal your information.

Cold Storage for Long-Term Investments:

If you're holding large amounts of cryptocurrency, store it in a hardware wallet (cold storage) rather than leaving it on an exchange. Exchanges can be hacked, and holding your funds in a personal wallet gives you full control and security.

Making Your First Purchase

Once your wallet is set up and you've chosen an exchange, you're ready to make your first cryptocurrency purchase. Here's a simple step-by-step guide:

Deposit Funds:

Most exchanges allow you to fund your account via bank transfer, credit card, or debit card. Some also support payments via PayPal or other payment services.

Choose a Cryptocurrency:

Decide which cryptocurrency you want to buy. For beginners, Bitcoin (BTC) and Ethereum (ETH) are popular starting points because they are widely accepted and have more stability compared to smaller altcoins.

Place an Order:

You can place a market order (which buys at the current market price) or a limit order (which buys when the cryptocurrency reaches a price you set).

Store Your Crypto:

Once the purchase is completed, transfer your cryptocurrency from the exchange to your personal wallet if you're planning on holding it long-term. Keeping your assets on the exchange can be riskier since exchanges are sometimes targeted by hackers.

Starting your journey into cryptocurrency investment involves a few key steps: setting up a secure wallet, choosing the right exchange, and adhering to strict security practices. While the process might seem complicated at first, these investments. With these basics in place, you're ready to start investing safely.

Now that you've set up your wallet and are ready to buy cryptocurrency, the next step is to develop a strategy for how you want to invest. There are several approaches to cryptocurrency investing, ranging from long-term holding to active trading. Now we'll explore the most common strategies and their benefits, so you can choose the one that best fits your financial goals and risk tolerance.

4
CRYPTO STRATEGY

The idea is simple: buy a cryptocurrency and hold it over a long period, regardless of short-term price fluctuations. This strategy works best for those who believe in the long-term growth of a cryptocurrency like Bitcoin or Ethereum.

How It Works:

Investors buy cryptocurrency and hold it for months or years, waiting for its value to increase over time.

The goal is to ignore short-term volatility and focus on the long-term potential of the asset.

Pros

Simple: Requires less monitoring and less active

trading.

Tax-efficient:

In some countries, holding crypto for more than a year can lower the tax rate on profits.

Reduced emotional trading:

HODLers are less likely to panic sell during market downturns, helping them avoid losses from emotional decisions.
Cons:

Volatility:

Short-term price drops can be stressful, especially if you need the money in the near term.

Missed opportunities:

HODLers may miss short-term *price spikes that could lead to profits.*

Best for:

Long-term investors who believe in the future of

major cryptocurrencies like Bitcoin and Ethereum.

Day Trading

For those looking for more active involvement, day trading involves buying and selling cryptocurrencies within short time frames, sometimes even within a single day, to profit from price fluctuations. This strategy is similar to stock day trading and requires a good understanding of the market, technical analysis, and the ability to react quickly.

How It Works:

Day traders monitor cryptocurrency prices closely, often using charts, trends, and indicators to predict short-term price movements. They execute multiple trades in a single day, aiming to make small profits with each trade.

Pros

High potential for profits:

Skilled traders can make significant profits in a short time.

Frequent opportunities:

Cryptocurrency markets are open 24/7, providing constant trading opportunities.

Cons

Time-consuming:

Requires constant monitoring and quick decision-making.

High risk:

The volatility of the market can lead to substantial losses if trades don't go as planned.

Technical knowledge required:

Successful day trading requires an understanding of chart patterns, market indicators, and trading psychology.

Best for:

Experienced investors with time to actively trade and strong knowledge of market trends and technical analysis.

Dollar-Cost Averaging (DCA):

Dollar-cost averaging (DCA) is a strategy where you invest a fixed amount of money into cryptocurrency at regular intervals (weekly or monthly), regardless of the market price. This strategy helps reduce the impact of volatility by spreading out your purchases over time.

How It Works:

Instead of trying to time the market and buy at the "best" price, you invest a set amount on a regular schedule.
When prices are low, your fixed amount buys more cryptocurrency. When prices are high, it buys less.

Pros

Reduces risk of timing the market:

By investing consistently, you avoid the risk of buying at a peak price.

Simple and passive:

DCA doesn't require constant monitoring or market analysis. Reduces emotional investment: You can stick to a set schedule, minimizing the stress of price fluctuations.

Cons

Misses opportunities for large gains:

DCA investors may not fully benefit from sharp price increases since they're not making large one-time purchases at low prices.

Small gains:

Since you're investing fixed amounts, it can take longer to see substantial returns.

Best for:

Beginners and long-term investors looking for a simple, low-stress way to accumulate cryptocurrency over time.

Staking and Earning Interest

Staking is a way to earn passive income on certain cryptocurrencies by holding and "staking" them in a network to support its operations (transaction validation on a Proof of Stake blockchain). In return, you earn rewards, typically in the form of additional cryptocurrency.

How It Works:

In Proof of Stake (PoS) networks like Ethereum 2.0, Polkadot, or Cardano, users can lock up (stake) their cryptocurrency to help validate transactions on the blockchain.
In return, stakers receive rewards, similar to earning interest in a traditional bank.

Pros

Earn passive income:

Staking allows you to earn additional cryptocurrency without actively trading.

Lower risk:

Staking is generally considered less risky than day trading since you're earning consistent rewards over time.

Supports the network:

By staking, you contribute to the security and stability of the blockchain.

Cons

Lockup period: Some staking platforms require you to lock up your assets for a fixed period, during which you can't access them.

Price volatility:

The value of the staked cryptocurrency can still drop, reducing the value of your rewards.

Best for:

Investors who prefer a more passive income strategy and plan to hold their cryptocurrencies for a longer period.

Yield Farming and Liquidity Providing:

Yield farming involves lending or staking your crypto currency in decentralized finance (DeFi) platforms to earn interest or rewards. Similarly, liquidity providing is the process of adding funds to decentralized exchanges (DEXs) like Uniswap to facilitate trading between users, earning a portion of the transaction fees in return.

How It Works:

Yield farmers lend their cryptocurrency to DeFi platforms or provide liquidity to DEXs, earning interest or a share of trading fees.
In return for providing liquidity, users receive liquidity tokens, which can sometimes be staked for additional rewards.

Pros:

High returns:

Some DeFi platforms offer much higher interest rates than traditional banks or even centralized crypto lending platforms.

Passive income:

Similar to staking, yield farming allows you to earn without active trading.

Cons:

Risk of loss:

If the value of the cryptocurrency you're lending or staking drops significantly, your earnings may not cover the loss.

Impermanent loss:

In liquidity providing, if the price of one token in the pair changes significantly, you could experience impermanent loss (losing value compared to holding the tokens outright).

Smart contract risks:

DeFi platforms rely on smart contracts, which can have vulnerabilities that hackers exploit.

Best for:

More experienced crypto users who understand DeFi risks and want to maximize returns through decentralized finance platforms.

Choosing the Right Strategy for You
When choosing an investment strategy, consider the following factors:

Time Commitment:

Day trading requires significant time and attention, while HODLing, staking, and dollar-cost averaging are more passive.

Risk Tolerance:

If you're risk-averse, you might prefer staking or dollar-cost averaging over high-risk strategies like day trading or yield farming.

Investment Goals:

If you believe in the long-term growth of a cryptocurrency, HODLing may be the best option. If you're looking for more frequent, short-term profits, day trading or yield farming might be more suitable.

There is no one-size-fits-all strategy when it comes to cryptocurrency investing. Whether you're looking for long-term growth, short-term gains, or passive income, there's a strategy that can fit your needs. The key is to choose one that aligns with your financial goals, time commitment, and risk tolerance.

5

Researching Cryptocurrencies

Investing in cryptocurrency isn't just about picking popular coins like Bitcoin or Ethereum; it's essential to understand the fundamentals behind each cryptocurrency.

How to Evaluate a Cryptocurrency

Before investing, it's important to do a thorough evaluation of any cryptocurrency. Here are some key factors to consider:

Market Capitalization:

Market capitalization (market cap) refers to the total value of a cryptocurrency. It's calculated by multiplying the current price by the total supply of coins in circulation.

Cryptocurrencies with a larger market cap (like Bitcoin and Ethereum) are generally considered more stable, while smaller market cap coins may offer higher rewards but come with more risk.

Tip: While market cap is important, a high market cap doesn't always mean the cryptocurrency is a good investment. It's crucial to look at other factors, too.

Trading Volume:

Trading volume indicates how much of a cryptocurrency is being bought and sold in a given period, usually 24 hours.

High trading volume suggests strong liquidity, meaning you can easily buy and sell the cryptocurrency without significantly affecting the price.

Supply and Demand

Total Supply:

How many coins will ever be created? Cryptocurrencies like Bitcoin have a limited supply (21 million), which creates scarcity and potentially increases demand over time.

Circulating Supply:

How many coins are currently in circulation? Some cryptocurrencies may have a large total supply but only a fraction of those coins are available for trading, which can impact price.

Understanding the Whitepaper

A whitepaper is a technical document released by a cryptocurrency project outlining its purpose, technology, and future plans. It's one of the most critical pieces of information when researching a cryptocurrency, as it explains the problem the project aims to solve and how it plans to do so.

What to Look for in a Whitepaper:

Use Case: Does the cryptocurrency solve a real-world problem? Does it offer something unique compared to existing coins?

Example: Bitcoin's use case is to provide a decentralized currency that isn't controlled by any government. Ethereum's use case is to enable smart contracts and decentralized applications (DApps).

Technology: What technology is the project using? Does it rely on a well-established blockchain like Ethereum, or is it using its own technology? Does the technology provide a clear advantage over competitors?

Roadmap: A good whitepaper will have a clear development roadmap, detailing when new features or improvements will be implemented.

Team: Who are the founders and developers behind the project? Do they have a strong track record in the tech or blockchain space? Transparency about the team's credentials is essential.

Tokenomics: How does the token function within the project? Is it just a currency, or does it have additional utility (governance rights, staking)?

Where to Find Whitepapers: You can usually find whitepapers on the official website of the cryptocurrency project or on trusted platforms like CoinMarketCap or CoinGecko.

Analyzing Use Cases and Technology

A cryptocurrency's value often depends on its use case and the underlying technology. These are key components that differentiate one coin from another.

Utility vs. Currency:

Currency Coins: Cryptocurrencies like Bitcoin are primarily used as a store of value or medium of exchange.

Utility Tokens: Many altcoins (Ethereum, Chainlink) serve specific functions within their ecosystems. For example, Ethereum enables smart contracts, while Chainlink facilitates decentralized oracles.

Real-World Applications:

The more a cryptocurrency can be used in real-world applications, the more likely it is to succeed. For example, Ethereum's ability to power decentralized finance (DeFi) applications has made it highly valuable.
Consider whether the cryptocurrency is solving

a significant problem or introducing an innovation that has real-world implications.

Blockchain Speed and Scalability:

One key metric to examine is how fast a blockchain can process transactions. Cryptocurrencies like Solana or Avalanche are known for their high speed and scalability, which makes them attractive for specific use cases (gaming, decentralized finance). Security Features:

Check the security measures implemented in the technology. Does the blockchain use Proof of Work (PoW), Proof of Stake (PoS), or another consensus mechanism? PoS, for example, is considered more energy-efficient and scalable than PoW.

Community and Development Activity

A cryptocurrency's community and developer activity are important indicators of its long-term potential. A strong community often drives the success of a project, while consistent developer activity ensures that the technology is being maintained and improved.

Developer Activity

Look at the project's GitHub or development repositories to see how frequently the code is updated. A project with ongoing updates is a good sign that the team is committed to improving and growing the technology.

Example: Ethereum consistently ranks among the top projects in terms of developer activity due to its active community of developers creating decentralized applications (DApps) and scaling solutions.

Community Support

Strong community engagement often signals that people believe in the project's vision. Check social media platforms like Reddit, Twitter, or Discord to gauge community sentiment.

Tip: Beware of projects that rely on hype and flashy marketing rather than real technological innovation or solid fundamentals.

Partnerships and Collaborations:

Established partnerships with reputable companies or other blockchain projects can add credibility to a cryptocurrency.

Example: Chainlink's partnerships with Google Cloud and Oracle have boosted its reputation and contributed to its growth.

Identifying Red Flags

While many cryptocurrency projects are legitimate, the industry has its fair share of scams and poorly executed projects. Here are some common red flags to look out for:

Lack of Transparency:

If the team behind the project is anonymous or their credentials are difficult to verify, this is a major red flag. Transparency about the team and their experience is critical for legitimacy.

Overhyped Marketing:

Projects that spend more time on marketing and hype rather than developing the actual product should be approached with caution. High promises of "guaranteed returns" or "the next

Bitcoin" are typically a sign of a scam.

Fake Partnerships:

Be wary of projects that claim high-profile partnerships that cannot be verified. Always double-check any partnership announcements through credible sources.

Poorly Written Whitepaper:

If the whitepaper is vague, full of buzzwords, or lacks clear technical explanations, it might be a sign that the project isn't well thought out. A good whitepaper should clearly explain the problem the project is solving, how it plans to do so, and what makes it unique.

No Clear Roadmap or Delays:

A project with no roadmap, or one that consistently misses deadlines, may lack direction or be poorly managed.

Proper research is essential before investing in any cryptocurrency. By understanding key factors like market cap, use case, technology, and community support, you can make informed decisions about which cryptocurrencies have the most potential for growth. Identifying red flags will also help you avoid scams and poorly managed projects. With this research approach, you're better prepared to evaluate cryptocurrencies and choose the best investment opportunities.

6

Managing Your Portfolio

Once you've started investing in cryptocurrencies, managing your portfolio is crucial to maximizing returns and minimizing risks. In this chapter, we'll cover how to diversify your investments, track performance, rebalance your portfolio, and develop an exit strategy.

Diversifying Your Investments

Diversification is one of the most effective strategies for managing risk in any investment portfolio. By spreading your investments across different assets, you reduce the risk of losing everything if one asset underperforms.

Why Diversification is Important

Cryptocurrencies are volatile, and some coins may perform very well while others may drop in value. Diversifying across multiple cryptocurrencies reduces your exposure to the risk of any single coin failing.

How to Diversify:

Large Cap Cryptocurrencies: These are the most established and widely traded, such as Bitcoin (BTC) and Ethereum (ETH). They are generally considered safer and less volatile, making them a solid foundation for any crypto portfolio.

Mid Cap and Small Cap Cryptocurrencies

These coins have smaller market capitalizations but may offer higher growth potential. Examples include Polkadot (DOT), Cardano (ADA), or Avalanche (AVAX). However, they can be riskier.

Stablecoins:

Tether (USDT), USD Coin (USDC), and other stablecoins are pegged to traditional currencies like the US Dollar. Including stablecoins in your portfolio can provide stability and liquidity during volatile market periods.

Decentralized Finance (DeFi) Tokens:

DeFi projects like Uniswap (UNI), Aave (AAVE), and Chainlink (LINK) are part of the growing decentralized finance ecosystem. Adding DeFi tokens can diversify your portfolio into different sectors of the crypto space.

Sector Diversification

Diversify not just across different cryptocurrencies but across different sectors within the crypto market, such as:

Payment Networks:

(Bitcoin, Litecoin)
Smart Contract Platforms: (Ethereum, Solana)

DeFi Tokens:

(Uniswap, Aave)
Metaverse and NFTs: (Decentraland, Axie Infinity)

Tracking Performance:

Once you've diversified your portfolio, it's important to monitor how your investments are performing over time. Fortunately, there are several tools and apps available that make tracking your crypto portfolio easy.

Popular Portfolio Tracking Tools

CoinMarketCap and CoinGecko:

 These websites provide real-time price tracking and allow you to build and monitor a portfolio of cryptocurrencies.

Blockfolio (FTX App):

 A mobile app designed for tracking cryptocurrency prices and managing your portfolio.

Delta:

Another portfolio management app that supports a wide range of cryptocurrencies and provides detailed analytics on your holdings.

Key Metrics to Monitor

Current Value:

The total market value of your crypto assets.

Price Changes:

Monitor price movements in your assets and watch for trends (Is a particular cryptocurrency steadily increasing or experiencing frequent drops?).

Overall Gains or Losses:

Compare your initial investment to its current value to understand whether you're gaining or losing over time.

Asset Allocation:

Keep track of how much of your portfolio is in each asset class (large cap, small cap, stablecoins) and ensure it aligns with your risk tolerance.

Rebalancing Your Portfolio

As the market changes, the value of your investments will fluctuate, causing the balance of your portfolio to shift. Rebalancing is the process of adjusting your portfolio to maintain your desired allocation of assets.

Why Rebalance?:

Over time, the percentage of your portfolio in certain assets may grow or shrink due to price changes. For example, if Bitcoin's price rises significantly while smaller altcoins decline, Bitcoin may make up a larger portion of your portfolio than you originally intended. Rebalancing helps you maintain your investment strategy and risk tolerance by selling overperforming assets and reinvesting in under performing ones.

How Often to Rebalance

Time-based Rebalancing:

Some investors rebalance their portfolios on a regular schedule, such as monthly or quarterly.

Threshold-based Rebalancing:

Others prefer to rebalance when an asset exceeds or falls below a certain threshold. For example, if Bitcoin grows from 40% of your portfolio to 60%, you might sell some Bitcoin to restore balance.

Risks of Not Rebalancing:

If you don't rebalance, you could become overly concentrated in one asset, increasing your exposure to risk. This could lead to larger losses if that asset declines sharply.

Exit Strategies:

Having an exit strategy is just as important as knowing when to buy. Whether you're holding long-term or trading short-term, having a plan for when to sell can help you avoid emotional decisions and maximize profits.

Types of Exit Strategies

Profit-Taking:

Set a target price or percentage gain where you plan to sell part or all of your holdings. This helps lock in profits while allowing you to continue participating in further potential growth.

Stop-Loss Orders:

A stop-loss order is a predefined price at which you sell a cryptocurrency to prevent further losses.

For example, if you bought Bitcoin at $30,000, you might set a stop-loss at $28,000 to limit your losses if the price drops.

Selling Gradually:

Rather than selling all at once, some investors prefer to sell in stages. This allows you to take some profits while leaving room for further upside.

Rebalancing as an Exit Strategy:

As part of rebalancing, you might choose to exit certain positions that have grown too large relative to your overall portfolio or that no longer fit your investment goals.

Factors to Consider When Exiting

Market Sentiment:

If the overall market sentiment is bearish (negative), you might consider reducing exposure to riskier assets.

Fundamental Changes:

Exit if there are fundamental changes in a cryptocurrency's technology, leadership, or regulatory environment that negatively affect its long-term prospects.

Personal Financial Goals:

Consider your personal financial goals. If you've reached your profit target or need to use the funds elsewhere, it might be time to sell.

Managing Emotional Investing

One of the biggest challenges in cryptocurrency investing is managing your emotions. The market's volatility can lead to fear-driven selling or greed-driven buying, both of which can negatively impact your returns.

Common Emotional Pitfalls:

Fear of Missing Out (FOMO):

Investors may rush to buy a cryptocurrency when it's rapidly increasing in price, often leading to buying at a peak.

Panic Selling:

In a downturn, some investors may panic and sell their assets at a loss, fearing that prices will never recover.

Tips for Managing Emotions:

Stick to Your Strategy: Having a clear strategy for buying, holding, and selling helps you make rational decisions, even when the market is volatile.

Focus on Long-Term Goals:

Remember why you invested in the first place and avoid making decisions based on short-term market fluctuations.

Use Automation:

Setting up automatic buying (using DCA) or stop-loss orders can help remove emotions from your decisions.

Managing your crypto portfolio is essential for maximizing returns and minimizing risk. By diversifying your investments, regularly tracking performance, rebalancing when needed, and sticking to a well-defined exit strategy, you can protect your assets and make informed decisions. Understanding and managing the emotional side of investing is equally important to avoid costly mistakes.

7

Staying Safe in the Crypto Space

While cryptocurrency offers exciting opportunities, the industry is also rife with scams, fraud, and security vulnerabilities. In this chapter, we'll explore how to stay safe in the crypto space by recognizing common scams, following best security practices, and understanding the regulatory landscape.

Avoiding Common Scams

Cryptocurrency is largely unregulated, which has unfortunately made it a target for scammers. Being aware of the most common scams can help you avoid losing your funds.

Phishing Attacks:

Phishing occurs when scammers trick you into revealing your private keys, login credentials, or other sensitive information by pretending to be legitimate websites or services.

How it works:

Scammers often send emails, messages, or set up fake websites that closely resemble popular crypto exchanges or wallet providers. If you enter your details, they can access your funds.

How to avoid it:

Always check the URL of the website you're using. Phishing sites often have slightly misspelled URLs or extra characters (Coinbase.com vs. coinbas3.com).

Never click on links from unsolicited emails or messages, even if they appear to come from legitimate services.

Ponzi and Pyramid Schemes:

These schemes promise high returns with little or no risk. In reality, they pay returns to early investors using the funds of new investors until the scheme collapses.

Red flags:

Promises of guaranteed returns, especially very high ones. Referral programs that focus more on recruiting new investors rather than actual investment performance. Lack of transparency about how the investment works.

Example: BitConnect was a Ponzi scheme that collapsed in 2018, causing investors to lose billions of dollars.

Fake ICOs and Rug Pulls:

An Initial Coin Offering (ICO) is a way for new cryptocurrency projects to raise funds. Some fraudulent projects conduct ICOs, collect money, and then disappear.

Rug pulls occur when developers create a cryptocurrency, hype it up to attract investors, and then suddenly withdraw all funds, leaving investors with worthless tokens.

How to avoid it:

Research the project's whitepaper, team, and community before investing.
Avoid projects that lack transparency or have anonymous developers.

Pump-and-Dump Schemes:

In these schemes, groups of traders coordinate to artificially inflate the price of a cryptocurrency (the "pump"), encouraging others to buy in. Once the price reaches a peak, they sell their holdings (the "dump"), causing the price to crash and leaving other investors with losses.

How to avoid it:

 Be wary of sudden price spikes, especially in lesser-known cryptocurrencies, and avoid investing based on hype or rumors in chat groups or social media.

Security Best Practices

Cryptocurrency transactions are irreversible, so it's crucial to follow strong security practices to protect your funds.

Use Two-Factor Authentication (2FA):

Always enable 2FA on your crypto exchange accounts and wallets. This adds an extra layer of security by requiring not only your password but also a verification code from an app like Google Authenticator or a text message. Avoid SMS-based 2FA when possible, as phone numbers can be hijacked through SIM swapping attacks.

Keep Your Private Keys Safe:

Your private key gives you access to your cryptocurrency. If someone else gets it, they can transfer your funds to their wallet, and you have no way of getting them back.

Never share your private key with anyone. Store it securely, either in a hardware wallet or written down and stored offline.

Cold Storage and Hardware Wallets:

For long-term storage, use a cold wallet (offline wallet) like a Ledger or Trezor hardware wallet. Cold storage keeps your private keys offline, safe from online attacks.

If possible avoid keeping large amounts of crypto on exchanges, as they are more vulnerable to hacks.

Use Reputable Exchanges:

Stick to well known and reputable cryptocurrency exchanges like Coinbase, Binance, or Kraken for your transactions. Avoid unknown or unregulated exchanges, especially those with limited security features or poor customer reviews.

Regularly Update Software:

Ensure that your wallet software and devices are always up to date. Software updates often include patches for security vulnerabilities.

Use a Password Manager:

Store your passwords in a password manager to avoid weak or reused passwords. Use long, complex passwords for all your accounts.

Regulatory Considerations

Cryptocurrency is still a relatively new and evolving industry, and regulations vary widely by country. Understanding the legal landscape where you live is essential to staying compliant and avoiding penalties.

Taxes on Cryptocurrency:

Many countries now consider cryptocurrency as property or assets, meaning they are subject to capital gains taxes. This applies when you sell, trade, or use cryptocurrency to buy goods or services.

Example: In the US, the IRS requires that you report all cryptocurrency transactions and pay taxes on profits. Even if you only hold crypto for investment purposes, you may owe taxes when you sell at a profit.

How to stay compliant:

Keep detailed records of all your cryptocurrency transactions, including the date, amount, and purpose of each transaction.

Use crypto tax software like CoinTracker or Koinly to help calculate and report your taxes.

Know Your Customer (KYC) and Anti-Money Laundering (AML) Regulations:

Many countries require cryptocurrency exchanges to follow KYC and AML regulations, meaning you must provide identification to trade. This helps prevent illegal activities like money laundering or terrorist financing.

Impact on privacy:

While KYC helps improve security, it also reduces privacy. Some decentralized exchanges (DEXs) don't require KYC, but they come with greater risks, including fewer legal protections. Bans and Restrictions:

Some countries have outright banned cryptocurrencies or imposed strict regulations on trading. For example, China has banned cryptocurrency trading and mining, while other countries like India are exploring ways to regulate the industry.

Impact on you:

If you live in a country with strict crypto laws,

you may face challenges when trying to buy, sell, or hold cryptocurrency legally. Always check your country's regulations before investing.

Protecting Against Hacks and Losses

Even if you follow best practices, it's still important to be prepared in case something goes wrong. Here are a few extra steps to safeguard against hacks or losses:

Back Up Your Wallet:

If you're using a software wallet, make sure to back it up regularly. Most wallets provide a recovery phrase or seed phrase, which allows you to recover your wallet if you lose access to it. Keep this phrase stored offline in a secure place.

Monitor Transactions:

Regularly check your accounts and wallet balances for any unauthorized transactions. If you spot suspicious activity, act immediately by transferring your funds to a new wallet or contacting your exchange's support team.

Beware of Public Wi-Fi:

Avoid accessing your crypto accounts on public Wi-Fi networks, as they can be easily compromised. If you must use public Wi-Fi, use a Virtual Private Network (VPN) for added security.

Set Spending Limits:

On many exchanges, you can set spending limits or withdrawal limits to reduce the risk of someone draining your account in the event of a hack.

Dealing with Fraud or Hacks:

If you fall victim to fraud or a hack, it's important to know what steps to take:

Contact the Exchange:

If your funds were stolen from an exchange, contact the platform's support team immediately. Some exchanges have insurance to cover losses from certain types of hacks.

Report to Authorities:

In some cases, especially with large amounts of stolen cryptocurrency, it may be appropriate to report the theft to local authorities or specialized agencies, like the FBI's Internet

Crime Complaint Center (IC3) in the US.
Learn from the Experience:

If you've been hacked or scammed, use it as a learning experience to strengthen your security practices. Ensure that you don't repeat the same mistakes, and educate others in the crypto community about potential risks.

Staying safe in the crypto space requires vigilance and awareness of common scams, strong security practices, and knowledge of the regulatory environment. By following the strategies outlined in this chapter—such as using cold storage, enabling two-factor authentication, and avoiding phishing schemes—you can significantly reduce your risks. In the final chapter, we'll look to the future of cryptocurrency and explore how you can stay informed about emerging trends.

8

Emerging Trends in Cryptocurrency

Several key trends are reshaping the cryptocurrency landscape. While it's impossible to predict the future with certainty, understanding these trends can help you spot new opportunities.

Decentralized Finance (DeFi):

DeFi aims to recreate traditional financial systems—such as lending, borrowing, and trading—using blockchain technology, without the need for banks or intermediaries.

Key DeFi Platforms:

Projects like Aave, Uniswap, and MakerDAO enable users to lend, borrow, and earn interest using cryptocurrency.

DeFi is one of the fastest-growing sectors in cryptocurrency. It provides a way for users to gain financial services in a decentralized, permissionless manner, often with higher yields than traditional finance.

Non-Fungible Tokens (NFTs):

NFTs are unique digital assets that represent ownership of specific items such as art, music, or virtual real estate. They are powered by blockchain technology and have become particularly popular in the art and gaming worlds.

Key Platforms:

OpenSea, Rarible, and Axie Infinity are major NFT marketplaces.

NFTs are bringing mainstream attention to blockchain technology, and the market for digital ownership is expanding rapidly. NFTs could also revolutionize industries like gaming, fashion, and even real estate.

Web 3.0 and Decentralized Internet:

Web 3.0 is the concept of a decentralized internet, where users have control over their data and content. Cryptocurrencies and blockchain technology are central to this vision.

Key Projects:

Filecoin and IPFS focus on decentralized file storage, while Helium works on decentralized wireless networks.

Web 3.0 could reshape how we interact with the internet, shifting power away from large tech companies and toward individuals.

Layer 2 Solutions:

As cryptocurrencies like Ethereum grow in popularity, scalability becomes a critical issue. Layer 2 solutions are protocols that operate on top of existing blockchains to improve transaction speed and reduce costs.

Key Examples:

Polygon (MATIC) and Lightning Network for Bitcoin.

These solutions are essential for increasing the usability of major blockchains, particularly as they scale to support more users and applications.

Central Bank Digital Currencies (CBDCs):

Governments around the world are exploring the development of CBDCs, which are digital versions of national currencies like the US Dollar or the Euro. Unlike decentralized cryptocurrencies, CBDCs are issued and controlled by central banks.

CBDCs could integrate digital currency into the mainstream financial system, potentially coexisting or competing with decentralized cryptocurrencies.

The Role of Institutional Investors

The involvement of institutional investors in the

cryptocurrency market is growing, and this could have a profound impact on the future of the industry.

Increasing Adoption by Institutions:
Large companies like Tesla, MicroStrategy, and Square have invested in Bitcoin, while major financial institutions like Fidelity and Grayscale offer cryptocurrency investment products.

Institutional investment brings greater credibility, liquidity, and stability to the cryptocurrency market. As more institutions adopt crypto, it's likely to become a more widely accepted asset class.

Bitcoin ETFs:

Exchange-Traded Funds (ETFs) allow investors to buy and sell cryptocurrency as part of a diversified fund through traditional stock exchanges. Several Bitcoin ETFs have been launched, particularly in countries like Canada and the US.

ETFs make cryptocurrency more accessible to traditional investors who prefer not to hold the underlying asset directly.

Regulatory Developments and Their Impact

The regulatory environment surrounding cryptocurrency is constantly evolving. Governments worldwide are grappling with how to regulate crypto assets without stifling innovation.

Global Regulatory Trends:

Some countries, like El Salvador, have embraced Bitcoin as legal tender, while others, like China, have imposed strict bans on cryptocurrency activities.

Regulation is a double-edged sword. Clear regulations can bring legitimacy and encourage wider adoption, but overly restrictive laws could stifle innovation and drive crypto activities underground.

Tax and Compliance:

As governments introduce more regulations, it's important to stay compliant with tax and anti-money laundering laws. Many countries are increasing their focus on cryptocurrency taxation.

Tip: Keep detailed records of all your transactions and consult with a tax advisor to ensure compliance with local laws.

How to Stay Informed:

The cryptocurrency market moves quickly, and staying informed is essential for making smart investment decisions. Here are some of the best ways to keep up with the latest trends and news.

Trusted News Sources:

Follow reputable cryptocurrency news platforms like CoinDesk, The Block, and Decrypt to stay updated on market trends, regulatory changes, and new projects.
Podcasts and YouTube Channels:

Podcasts:

Shows like The Pomp Podcast and Unchained feature in-depth interviews with crypto experts, entrepreneurs, and regulators.

YouTube:

Channels like Coin Bureau and DataDash offer educational content and market analysis for crypto investors.

Social Media and Community Platforms:

Twitter and Reddit are two of the most active platforms for cryptocurrency discussions.
Follow key influencers, developers, and analysts for real-time updates.
Join Telegram and Discord groups for individual projects to stay connected with their communities and development progress.

Track Developer Activity:

Platforms like GitHub allow you to track developer contributions to cryptocurrency projects. Consistent development activity is a positive sign that the project is actively being improved.

Long-Term Outlook for Cryptocurrency

The future of cryptocurrency is full of potential, but it also faces challenges. Here are a few possible scenarios for how the industry might evolve in the coming years.

Mainstream Adoption:

As cryptocurrencies and blockchain technology become more integrated into our daily lives, we could see widespread adoption in areas such as banking, healthcare, and supply chain management. Cryptocurrencies like Bitcoin could also become a global store of value, similar to gold.

Integration with Traditional Finance:

The rise of central bank digital currencies (CBDCs) and more regulatory clarity could lead to a closer integration between crypto and traditional finance. Banks may start offering more crypto-related services, while blockchain technology could streamline financial transactions.

Innovation and New Use Cases:

Beyond financial applications, blockchain technology could revolutionize industries such as gaming (through NFTs), real estate (smart contracts), and governance (decentralized voting systems). The potential for innovation is vast.

Challenges and Risks:

The industry still faces significant hurdles, such as regulatory uncertainty, scalability issues, and environmental concerns (especially with Proof of Work cryptocurrencies like Bitcoin). How these challenges are addressed will shape the future of crypto.

The future of cryptocurrency is filled with possibilities, from the rise of DeFi and NFTs to the increasing involvement of institutional investors. By staying informed about emerging trends and regulatory developments, you can position yourself to take advantage of new opportunities and mitigate risks. As the crypto landscape continues to evolve, being proactive and adaptable will be key to long-term success.

Final Thoughts

Investing in cryptocurrency can be a rewarding but risky endeavor. Throughout this guide, we've covered everything from the basics of crypto to advanced strategies for managing your portfolio and staying safe. As you move forward in your crypto journey, remember that knowledge and preparation are your best allies.

THE
END

HOPE YOU ENJOYED
THIS BOOK AND IT HELPS YOU

THANK YOU VERY MUCH,
BECAUSE WITHOUT YOU THERE
ARE NO BOOKS